Flower Garden with Butterflies by U.S. Glass Company, late 1920s. Shown are several of the nine colors in which these highly decorative pieces were made. *Courtesy of Neil McCurdy.*

Floral by Jeannette Glass Company, 1931-1935. The lovely Poinsettia motif gives this pattern its nickname and makes it a perfect choice for a Christmas table.

Homespun by Jeannette Glass Company, 1938-1940.
The child's tea set was made in pink and crystal.

Iris by Jeannette Glass Company, 1928-1932, iridescent in 1950 & 1969. An interesting assortment of bowls, including this flower bowl, is available.

Floragold by Jeannette Glass Company, 1950s. Primarily an iridescent pattern, some pieces can be found in crystal (clear) and shell pink. *Courtesy of Marie Talone.*

English Hobnail by Westmoreland Glass Company, 1928-1950, crystal and amber until 1983. Made in a rainbow of colors, Jadite is the most elusive color of all. *Courtesy of Ruth Farrington.*

Fortune by Hocking Glass Company, 1936-1937. No dinner plates were made in this pattern that provides the pieces necessary to serve dessert or lunch. *Courtesy of Neil McCurdy & Staci & Jeff Shuck.*

Emerald Crest by Fenton Art Glass Company, 1949-1955. Shown is one of the many Fenton "Crests." *Courtesy of John & Jane & Jessica Schleinzer.*

Doric and Pansy by Jeannette Glass Company, 1937-1938. The child's tea set was sold as "Pretty Polly Party Dishes." *Courtesy of Neil McCurdy.*

Diana by Federal Glass Company, 1937-1941. The candy jar is the only lidded piece of Diana. *Courtesy of Marie Talone.*

Colonial, "Knife and Fork" by Hocking Glass Company, 1934-1938. A plethora of goblets and tumblers are available in pink, green, and crystal (clear).

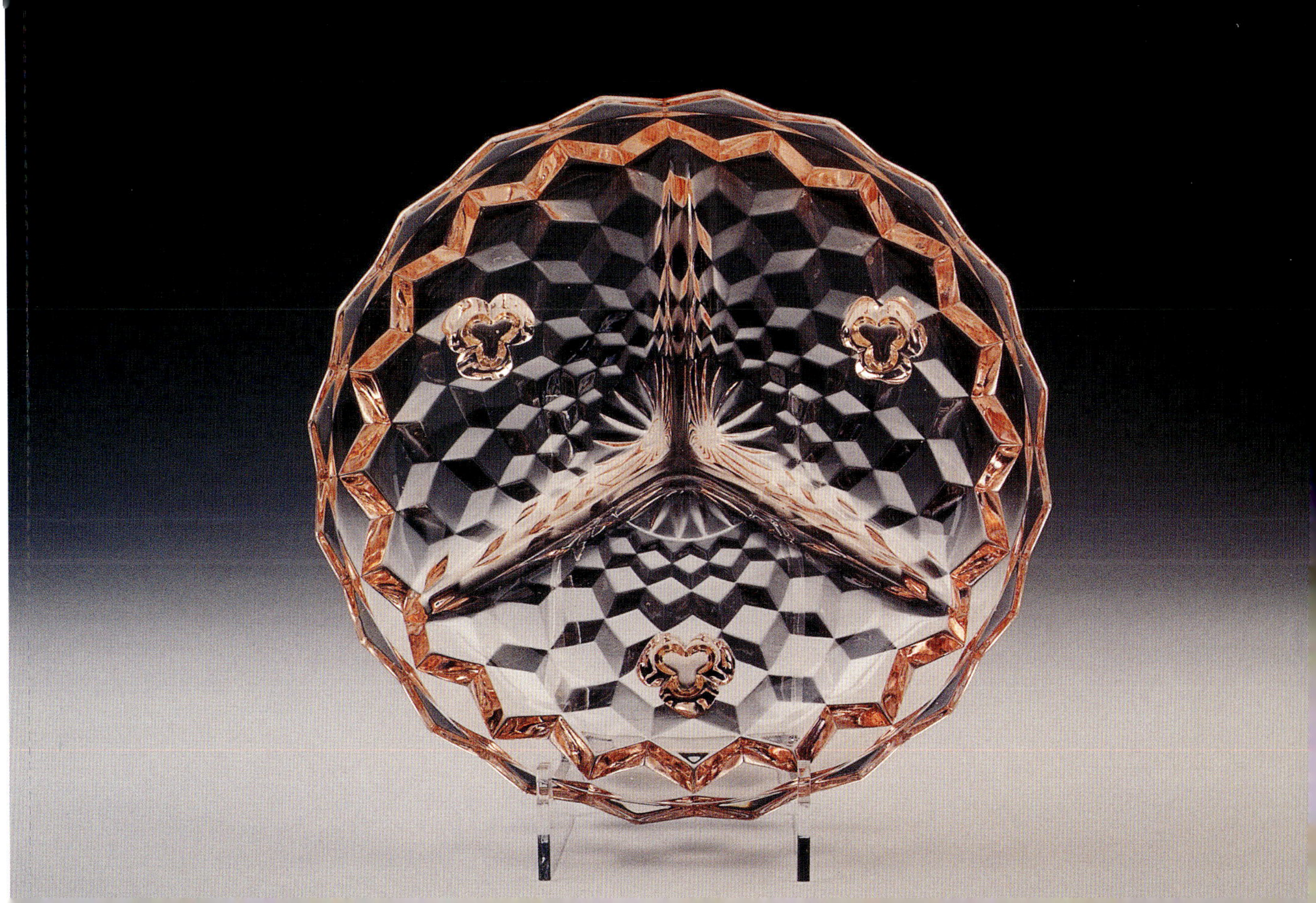

Cube by Jeannette Glass Company, 1929-1933. This three-footed relish is extremely rare. *Courtesy of Staci & Jeff Shuck.*

Dancing Nymph by Consolidated Glass Company, 1926-1939. This pattern exemplifies the Deco influence on Depression Era dinnerware.

Swirl by Jeannette Glass Company, 1937-1938. Found in pink and greenish blue, the ultramarine color shown here is the most popular color. *Courtesy of Michael Rothenberger.*

Adam by Jeannette Glass Company, 1932-1934. Adam is one of the few patterns offering square plates.

Mayfair by Hocking Glass Company, 1931-1936. Yellow pieces of Mayfair are particularly elusive. *Courtesy of Donna L. Cehlarik.*

Anniversary by Jeannette Glass Company, 1947-1949 with some pieces from the 1960s and 1970s. Jeannette Glass Company called this color "Amberescence."

Patrician by Federal Glass Company, 1933-1937. Patrician offers a complete set of dinnerware including these butter dishes. *Courtesy of Michael Rothenberger.*

American Pioneer by Liberty Works, 1931-1934. This well-made pattern offers a huge assortment of interesting pieces including four lamps and seven plates. *Courtesy of Staci & Jeff Shuck.*

Crow's Foot by Paden City Glass Company, 1930s. Found in many colors, this deep emerald green is particularly rare. *Courtesy of Marie Talone.*

Pyramid by Indiana Glass Company, 1928-1932. Strong angles characterize this hard-to-find pattern. *Courtesy of Marie Talone.*

Old Café by Hocking Glass Company, 1936-1938. This candy dish features the rare pairing of pink and Royal Ruby.

Ovide by Hazel-Atlas Glass Company, 1930-1935. The colors shown here are fired-on; the colors have been applied to white glass. *Courtesy of Kimberley & Walter Lemiski.*

Pebble Optic by Federal Glass Company, 1927-1932. Pebble Optic has only nineteen pieces, and seven of them are tumblers.

Orchid by Paden City Glass Manufacturing Company, 1929-1930s. Dramatic colors and pieces describe this elegant pattern. *Courtesy of Debora & Paul Torsiello.*

Jubilee by Lancaster Glass Company, 1930. Most Depression Glass patterns have designs molded into the glass, but Jubilee's flowers are cut into high quality glassware.

Moroccan Amethyst by Continental Can, 1960s. This pattern is found in many shapes; shown are swirled pieces. *Courtesy of Scott & Rhonda Hackenberg.*

Old English by Indiana Glass Company, 1926-1929. There are no plates in this pattern that offers mostly serving pieces. *Courtesy of Ted Bradley.*

Moderntone by Hazel-Atlas Glass Company. The plethora of Moderntone colors is shown in these salt and pepper shakers. *Courtesy of Michael Rothenberger.*

Moondrops by New Martinsville Glass Manufacturing Company, 1932-1940s. Dramatic detailing and bold colors are signature New Martinsville characteristics. *Courtesy of Debora & Paul Torsiello.*

Katy by Imperial Glass Company, 1930s. All pieces are trimmed with opalescent edges.

Beaded Block by Imperial Glass Company, 1927-1930s. A huge assortment of colors and variations can be found in this popular pattern. *Courtesy of Neil McCurdy.*

Coronation by Hocking Glass Company, 1936-1940. This stemmed sherbet and pitcher are among the most elusive pieces of Coronation. *Courtesy of Kyle & Barbara Ewing.*

Sharon by Federal Glass Company, 1935-1939. Shown are butter dishes in the three most collected colors of Sharon. *Courtesy of Michael Rothenberger.*

Wig-Wam by L.E. Smith Glass Company, 1930s. This console set was made in cobalt blue and pink.

Sandwich by Anchor Hocking Glass Company, 1940s-1960s.
Forest Green pitchers in this pattern are rare and expensive.
Courtesy of Wes & Carla Davidson.

White Ship by Hazel-Atlas Glass Company, late 1930s. Hazel-Atlas used "Ritz Blue" glass to create dramatic barware, dinnerware, and occasional pieces. *Courtesy of Bob & Cindy Bentley.*

Twisted Optic by Imperial Glass Company, 1927-1930. This console set is a small part of a pattern made in many colors in a vast assortment of pieces. *Courtesy of James Retzloff.*

Sierra by Jeannette Glass Company, 1931-1933. It is easy to see why this pattern has the nickname "Pinwheel."

Florentine No. 2 by Hazel-Atlas Glass Company, 1932-1935. The design on these candlesticks shows why this pattern is also called "Poppy." *Courtesy of Marie Talone.*